THE REAL ART OF TR~~

A Metamorphic Adventure into

the Possibilities of YOU & Us!

By Soleira Green

Who are you REALLY? An ordinary person with problems to solve? Or an extraordinary flow of potential and possibilities being fulfilled through you?

I've been fascinated with the art of transformation for the last 25 years. By transformation I don't mean just becoming a better person or learning to fulfil the potential that's already sitting within you. I'm talking about full blown breakthrough transformation ... a metamorphosis that leaps you from a small person with problems to solve to an amazing being with incredible contribution to make.

The real art of transformation is about ...

* empowering people to be the best they can be and then some!
* going beyond the fulfilment of potential into the realms of genius creation.
* helping others to make their lives count on an awesome scale.

*   coloring up Life with new ideas for people and the world to thrive upon.

I recommend you move through this adventure, one day at a time, absorbing a section or two each day, giving yourself time to let the transformational aspects of it settle in with you. On the other hand, if you're feeling like a horse at the starting gate, ready to roll into your greatest potential, then feel free to dive in fully all in one go!

About me, your guide on the transformational journey: I'm a visionary and genius enthusiast with a vision to unleash 7 billion geniuses co-creating a genius world. You can see how this adventure fits right into that vision! If you want to know more about me, my visions and my work, go to www.soleiragreen.com www.thegeniuscompany.co   www.thevisionarynetwork.com

TABLE OF CONTENTS

Introducing the Real Art of Transformation
Celebrating the transformation of you and us!

TRANSFORMING YOURSELF
Day 1: Your Transformational Tools
Day 2: What do you want to transform into?
Day 3: Celebrating the brilliant awesomeness of YOU!
Day 4: How to get to the MORE'ness of YOU.
Day 5: Touching the MORE'ness. Bursting the chrysalis.
Day 6: If you listen, you can hear yourself being called.
Day 7: Walking around as the MORE'ness of YOU!

TRANSFORMATIVE POWERS / ABILITIES
Day 8: New transformative abilities to power up your life
Day 9: Transformative Power #1 ~ The Power of Knowing
Day 10: Transformative Power #2 ~ The Power of Emotion
Day 11: Transformative Power #3 ~ The Power of Seeing
Day 12: Transformative Power #4 ~ The Power of Connection
Day 13: Transformative Power #5 ~ The Power of Exhilarating
Day 14: Transformative Power #6 ~ The Power of Genius Creation
Day 15: Transformative Power #7 ~ The Power of Consciousness Creation

TRANSFORMING OUR WORLD

Day 16: A Brand New Us!

Day 17: Creating Reality (your own) / Sourcing Reality (the world's)

Day 18: Our Metamorphic Future!

Day 19: The Transcendent YOU!

Day 20: Riding the Waves of Living Force

Day 21: Seeding the Gems of Wonder

Completing the adventure

Note: Images purchased from www.123rf.com

Celebrating the transformation of you & us!

There's transformation and there's TRANSFORMATION! Sometimes transformation is becoming more of who you already are and sometimes TRANSFORMATION is a complete remake of the possibilities of YOU!

I believe we're all going through a metamorphic TRANSFORMATION right now! As a race of beings on a genius planet, we're expanding our horizons, allowing ourselves the freedom to express who we really are, and coming into an exhilarated knowing of ourselves that is FAR beyond how we've known ourselves before.

How would you know if you're on that journey?

- The old ways won't work for you anymore as you push yourself into the NEW.
- You might be more energetically sensitive or get ill more often.
- You might be losing hold of your definition of you.
- You may burst into tears with no explanation or have moments of brilliance flash into you.

The transformation game can be a bit bumpy along the way, so let's look first in our 21 day adventure at 2 simple steps to PUT GRACE INTO YOUR METAMORPHIC JOURNEY ...

1. Know without a shadow of a doubt that you are a wondrous, unique creation ... that there is no other like you. Forget your history and your learning and always know you are awesome beyond compare!

2. Allow yourself to morph with great ease. Holding on to how you think you are or how you should be will always rock the transformation boat! Be thrilled by being able to reinvent and redefine yourself regularly.

Something is being called for from us in the 21st century. Can you feel it? A new urging, a wild becoming, a metamorphic potential. Let's see if we can co-create that urging into something brilliantly awesome for ourselves and for this wonderful world over the next 21 days!

GETTING READY FOR SPECTACULAR! For me, the real art of transformation is turning your life into SPECTACULAR'ness in every way. Looking forward to leaping into spectacular play with you throughout this journey!

Day 1

Your Transformational Tools

What tools do you need to pack for the adventure?

Tool #1: A SENSE OF HUMOR. Don't take things all seriously and significantly. Relax, have a laugh. It all turns out brilliant in the end.

Tool #2: A SENSE OF ADVENTURE. Don't stick to the trodden path. Set your transformational compass for the unknown and discover a world of wonder that lies just beyond the old you.

Tool #3: YOUR PAINTBRUSH OF CREATION. In the game of transformation, you are making yourself up at every moment in time. You are not who you've always been. You're a creational whirlpool of new possibilities just waiting to be painted into being.

Tool #4: A CLEAR BLANK CANVAS OF POSSIBILITY. Don't limit yourself with any previous knowing of yourself. Everything is possible for you. All gifts and abilities are yours for the asking, so plant yourself in the limitless, unfenced garden of creation.

Tool #5: A transformational buddy. Bring a friend along with you on the journey ... someone you trust and who's willing to allow you to unfold into limitless creation. Someone who can join you on the adventure and have a laugh together if the going gets tough.

Ready to roll on your transformational journey? **Today, day one, think of one new thing you'd love to be and spend today energising, playing with, and celebrating that it's already done and there for you.**

Day 2

What do you want to transform into?

When I wrote day 1 as a post on Facebook, someone shared it looking for a transformational buddy. A wonderful man posted back *'Transform into what?'* She replied *'Anything you want.'* and he came back with *'A frog for kissing!'* I loved it and I thought how apt that was for day two's adventure.

WHAT DO YOU WANT TO TRANSFORM INTO?

I see three distinct levels of transformation:

(1) Into the you that's always been waiting inside, like the prince in the frog, ready to pop out with the right incentive.

(2) Into you as a greater being with a greater purpose, like the great leader / king the prince has yet to become.

(3) Into limitless possibility as your own creation -- what if the prince doesn't want to be a prince or a king, but instead he yearns to be the best kisser in the land to awaken all the fair maidens into their true transformation ... a transformer extraordinaire!

Let me show you this in a more practical and real example. I watched 'The Unteachables' tv show, a special project to show that kids with bad behaviour at school can be transformed into great learners. This one young man, Zaak, burst into tears when for the first time ever his special teacher wrote in his report that he was a genius. Then when Zaak had the opportunity to be a teaching assistant for a day with young children, he wow'd everyone by taking each child up to the front of the class and singing their praises, inviting the whole class to be a team and support every player.

Now because of the frog prince's kiss (his teacher), Zaak just might turn into a great teacher (a frog prince himself— level 1). Or more than that, he just might become the one to transform every child in the land with a new kind of genius education (level 2). Or he might surprise us all by becoming the world's greatest genius ensuring that people the world over are praised, celebrated, and transformed (level 3). Go Zaak!

What do you want to transform into today?

Let the limitless creation begin! Kiss, kiss!

Day 3

Celebrating the awesomeness of you!

Ok, so you've packed your backpack with your transformational tools and you've created the map for who you want to become. Next we're going to do an assessment of who you are now that will transform your view of yourself. Ready, set, go....

1. **What one thing do you do better than anyone else in the world?**

2. **What do you love most about yourself?**

3. **What's the biggest gift you have given to the world in your life so far?**

I'm asking you these questions so that you can **ORIENT YOURSELF TO YOUR WONDERFUL, AWESOME, GENIUS SELF** -- because it's hard to transform when you're not in full appreciation of who you already are.

Most people get down on themselves pretty regularly. But the transformational journey requires that you skip that bit. Transformation doesn't happen by processing issues, clearing blocks, or assessing your flaws. Transformational power soars into play when you are in the full jubilant joy of who you already are with a willingness to become more and more and more!

Yes, I know -- loads of transformation happens by losing yourself and that can often be associated with negative assessments of one's capacity. But to put real grace and power in your transformational adventure, **WE'RE GOING FOR THE BRILLIANT AWESOME'NESS OF YOU AS THE STARTING POINT FOR THE ADVENTURE!**

So come on folks, celebrate your wonderfulness. Let your vibration soar and allow yourself to be in the full flow and joy of you today as we take the next steps into the metamorphic transformation of you and us!

Day 4

How to get to the MORE'NESS of you.
Let the universe whisper its dreams in your ear!

It's day 4 of our transformational adventure! Here we go onto the next step together: How can you get to the more'ness of you? I see three levels of play here:

(1) THE NORMAL YOU -- Who you've always been and how you know yourself now. It's how you've been shaped by the history, the learning, the upbringing, and the life experiences of you.

(2) THE POTENTIAL YOU -- The unique contributions that sit inside you just waiting to pop out into the world. It's the passions, the essence, and the uniqueness of you coming out to play!

(3) THE MORE'NESS OF YOU -- The creation of yourself as limitless possibility becoming more and more real every day. This is beyond how you know yourself and beyond what's already built into you. It's the evolution of us and Life! It's what you haven't even dreamed you can be yet -- but it's waiting there in the limitless universe of Creation holding out its hand to you, whispering its dreams in your ear.

Below are two examples of universal whispers of possibility that I did for some people recently:

You walk in gardens of sunlight with moonbeams dancing throughout. There is no one on this world who can shine like you can, who can illuminate the darkness with brilliant sparkling insights into sovereign creation. The pathways to wonder open before you, leaving people breathtaken in its wake. There is so much more for you yet to bring through, so much you have yet to direct them all to. You are a voice for the unknown. What will be left when you are gone will be a world in awe of your creations. Walk boldly great sensai.

Translation: A transformative teacher of new ways of living, working, and playing.

You open the doorways into vast new playgrounds of possibility. A queen amongst the stars, you call all the princes and princesses to come forth, to create and collaborate together that which has never been before. You teach them how to be great, awesome, wondrous. You call their greatness from the great beyond and pour it into the fabric of them. Yet there is more. Your legacy is one of royal wonder....that every single living being is a leader, a queen, a king, a prince and princess in waiting to lead the world into its most profound becoming. To get us ready for a pathway unknown, an adventure so charmed and enchanting that each will awaken with their most glorious contributions ready to give into the collective Creation. The Earth shudders with excitement at your every breath as the universe breathes its power through you for our imminent becoming!

Translation: Birthing a new kind of leadership in the world.

Day 5

TOUCHING THE MORE'NESS

BURSTING THE CHRYSALIS

I hope you enjoyed letting the universe whisper its dreams in your ear. While it can sound a bit poetic in that form, it's also important to realise that said that way, it touches something really deep within, like something you've known forever and yet not ever known in this lifetime.

If you're looking for your MORE'ness, stop thinking about it, stop trying to find your purpose in the normal ways, and let yourself go deep into the feeling of it. Let a wave of the profound surge up from inside you, touching the fabric of you as you emerge from the cocoon to become something extraordinary.

Human beings tend to walk around in life trying to know themselves and yet some of the finest geniuses, the most awesome beings show up when you let go of the you you know and surrender into the arms of greatness ... the profound stirring of possibility which is waiting for us all to breath into creation.

To truly transform you need to touch that profound place that lies like a seed within each and every one, just waiting to burst into bloom. That moment will often call forth a springing of tears and then whoosh the potent alchemical rush moves through that person transforming them forever into that which Life wants them to become! The chrysalis bursts free and the awesome being emerges from its cocoon to wow the Universe in Creation!

And the good news is that once you've said yes to the MORE, all pathways lead to enwonderment!

Day 6

If you listen, you can hear yourself being called!

How are you doing on our transformational adventure? Are you beginning to look at yourself differently? Finding new possibilities for who you can be and what you can be up to?

I can imagine that for some our conversation around MORE'ness is a bit of a leap, while for others it's the breath they breathe, always yearning to feel the calling into the next great contribution that awaits!

Why is it that some yearn to be called while others often don't even notice it when it's banging on their door? Can everyone become the MORE that is waiting for us right now?

My answer to that is YES! And sometimes people get caught up in the 'normal' things in life and miss the universe whispering in their ears. So how can you attune to the whispers, hear the calling, and follow the pathway (in a very practical sense) into the MORE'ness of you?

ATTUNING TO THE WHISPERS

The universe, Life, the creative oomph, genius flow ... whatever you'd like to call it ... is always pulsing new possibilities towards us. To listen to them you have to attune to its frequency. Here's how I do it: Think of something you love to put you in the good feeling, high vibe. Next reach out to make a relationship with Life. This is a feeling experience, not a thinking experience, although feel free to imagine it as that works too. Now tune your sensory antennae to the creative urgings that are swimming all around us just waiting for someone to pluck them from the genius fields. It's just like turning the radio dial till you get the station / music you like.

HEARING THE CALLING

Next you want to suspend the mind. That means *'Don't think. Listen.'* The MORE'ness whispers and urgings are a feeling that comes to you ... a trickle of energetic delight that flows towards you. Make friends with it. Say hello and invite it to sit down with you for a chat. Then imagine you're talking with the universe and listen to what it has to say to you. Don't assess it or judge it while listening. Just let it flow as it charms you with its wonder.

FOLLOWING THE PATHWAY

Once you've chatted and plucked the new possibility from the field of flow, you want to interpret it in a practical way for yourself so you can determine if you're going to say yes to this possibility or not. If it's a YES, be sure to let the universe / Life know, then ask for some specific guidelines as to how to put that into practical reality for yourself. You'll be amazed just how brilliantly strategic the universe / Life can be when you ask for the practical how to's. And then, pick the practical action you like the most and start! Do one thing today towards that, setting it in motion to be realised in reality!

Day 7

Walking around as the MORE'ness of You!

Let the genius universe flow through you.

As you can see, we're now moving into making this new / more YOU a practical, real life, walking, talking specimen of MORE'ness. How can you make that real and sustainable in your everyday life? Here are some great daily exercises to help make that so:

(1) When you wake up every morning, remind yourself that you are a breath of possibility walking. Breathe the next possibility of you in and exhale the reality of that possibility out into the world.

(2) Keep yourself in a good high vibe. Think of something you love. Do something you love. Laugh. Be in awe of the flowers in bloom. Put some 10 second exercises into place throughout your day where you're playing in this vibe until it becomes a sustainable energetic reality for you.

(3) Ask your transformational buddy to 'see' you as the MORE'ness. The more we're seen, the more we show up as it in life. Make sure that you're hanging out with people who really get you and want to see only the very best in you and for you all the time.

(4) And finally, let the genius universe flow through you at least once a day. Everyone will do that differently. Me I type it. Others will sing it, dance it, paint it, breathe it, garden it, etc. It's this last tip that will REALLY have you discover and show up as the MORE'ness of YOU!

Day 8

Transformative Abilities to Power Up Your Life!

Twenty-five years ago when I started on my own transformational journey, I thought that the ability to power my own life and the world's potential was a wisp of a dream unlikely to be achieved in my lifetime. Hah! How little did I know that it would come so easy and so fast to us all.

Today, we operate within a new energetic system, one that powers from the connected super core and operates with the limitless energy of a universe in creation. We dance in amongst the spaces of creation with great ease, sourcing reality into what we dream it can become. We can tune in to one another across the airwaves, to gain a richer, deeper understanding of human behaviour and the potential it offers. We can energise spaces for brilliance, genius, and magical outcomes to show up as the fulfilment of potential.

Of course each one of us will have unique abilities, but there is also the power of new super abilities now available for all. So let's go shopping for what you'd love to have as your new super abilities:

(1) The power of knowing: This comes from plugging in to the streaming flow of infinite intelligence, like a grand internet of genius intelligence that swims all around us. You have only to drop the thinking mind and let the knowing flow into and through you.

(2) The power of emotion: What if emotion is our friend versus our foe? We no longer need to process what's wrong with us or our past in order to use the powerful energy of emotion to transform into our next level of potential.

(3) The power of connecting: When you get into the high vibe (think of something you love and you're there), you connect with the awe and wonder of Life, of people, of the potential of circumstance, and suddenly find you have the ability to turn them out in genius new ways.

(4) The power of exhilarating: We can aliven (that means to bring something really ALIVE) people, situations, businesses, homes, opportunities, — sourcing the exhilaration and excitement of the NEW falling graciously into place.

(5) The power of seeing: As we see beyond what is, our alchemical transformative eyes can unleash the genius that's sitting within everyone and every moment. It's about learning to see beyond, into the realms of limitless possibility, super charging it with Life and drawing it graciously into living reality.

(6) The power of genius creation: We are creators now, able to create the consciousness of new reality, sentiencizing it into brilliant partnerships that work for the betterment of Life everywhere.

These abilities used to be a yearning and a dream for me. Now, for me and my buddies, they're a normal part of our everyday lives, filling us with the richness of fulfilment in playing a part in a world in motion towards its genius future! How about you? What are your new super abilities?

Day 9

TRANSFORMATIVE POWER #1:

The Power of Knowing

The power of knowing comes from plugging in to the streaming flow of infinite intelligence, like a grand internet of genius intelligence that swims all around us. You have only to drop the thinking mind and let the knowing flow into and through you.

Knowing is a brilliant way of superceding trained thinking, learned behaviour, and those ever so invisible cultural whispers that take us in the wrong direction every time!

The power of knowing lets you access a deep, profound, and expansive understanding of ...

(1) why things are happening as they are,
(2) what the potential of a circumstance is, and
(3) where you're heading next in your life!

While super powerful, the power of knowing is actually a baby step on the road to GENIUS. Genius streams through you, the same as knowing, to uplift life, to enrich possibility, to transform everyone and everything it touches. Both require you to surrender the thinking mind and allow yourself to be in a great relationship with the streaming flows of infinite intelligence and genius possibilities that dance all around us.

Let's test it out shall we ... the transformative power of knowing. Ask a question about something you're wanting to transform and then plug into the flow of knowing and see what you get. You want to practice this with all kind of scenarios and see just how transformative the power of knowing can be.

Day 10

TRANSFORMATIVE POWER #2:

The Power of Emotion

Years ago I believed that emotion had me and I was trying my hardest not to have it. Not to be angry, frustrated, or fearful. Trying to be mature and responsible. But then EUREKA! One day I realised I had it all backwards! These emotions are my very smart body's way of sending me the energy of movement ... anger as the tip of passion, fear as the excitement for the next big step, frustration as an indicator to get a move on girl! So I started to use the powerful energy of emotion as a pathway to my potential.

But then, wow, much to my surprise, as I began to relate to it this way, I discovered yet another layer of power within these genius emotions. The ability to light up the universe with them and power transformation and creation into the game of Life! Amazing!

So how can an emotion like fear, anger, or frustration, be utilised for the power of transformation and creation?

First, stop assuming that there's something wrong with you because you have one of these fabulous energetic bursts. That's the cultural whispers of psychology trapping you into your past for resolution. Instead shift your perspective and see this emotional energy as your friend instead of your foe, as your genius rather than your past issues, as the power of transformation offering out its hand to you instead of some yuck surfacing to be gotten rid of or dampened down.

Next, take a deep breath and get in relationship with the power of the energy. **Then ask from your knowing what is the potential of this for me ... and for the greater game for the world.** In fact you might start with orienting to the greater game potential first as that unlocks the door from personal into profound contribution.

Once you've got a sense of what this is for, then power the energy through for that purpose ... et voila, you'll discover in the process that you are transformed and have moved to your own next level of genius play!

Day 11

TRANSFORMATIVE POWER #3:

The Power of Seeing

I believe that the greatest gift you can give anyone is to SEE who they really are. It's one of the most transformative things you can do for a person.

It's not about looking with 'normal' eyes. It's about seeing beyond what is, beyond the learned behaviour and the created identity into the very essence and greatness of a person.

ESSENCE is the essential qualities of you. Distilled down to an extract of wonder, essence is that elixir of awesomeness that makes you up from the inside out. It's what makes you unique from all other beings everywhere! It's your signature that gets danced into the universe to bring delicious diversity to the game.

GREATNESS is the possibility of you. More than potential, greatness is about surrendering the you you know to dance with the limitless gems of genius that the universe is powering towards you.

In other words, essence is the unique you and greatness is the YOU you have yet to become! Using transformative eyes, you can bring both powering into the game.

HOW TO POWER GREATNESS WITH TRANSFORMATIVE EYES:

1. First you want to 'unknow' that person. Come on, you already 'know' how they are. You have to forget all that, as if it's an illusion, a costume, that's not the real deal them. By unknowing them, you're opening up to the possibility they can be.

2. Next, you want to connect with that person in a deep / profound and vast / expansive way. For essence, it's as if you're getting to recognise their true signature blend that wafts wonder into the cosmos. For greatness, it's as if you step way way back to allow the vastness of them to soar into reality.

3. Then use your transformative eyes to see the brilliance and genius of them into reality. You're an artist painting a portrait of them as they've never seen themselves before. You bask in the awe and wonder of them. You revel in the delight they bring and the greatness they are about to unfold.

4. Finally, you call their greatness to them and see it into gracious becoming as their enormous contribution to our world. The more you can hold the knowing of their greatness, the more they become it graciously now.

Try this with someone you know and love. It's especially easy to do with children because they haven't defined their costume yet and are still essence pouring into Life with greatness swirling through their being. May you be seen and see the world as awesome today!

Day 12

TRANSFORMATIVE POWER #4:

The Power of Connection

When you transformatively connect with someone, you're connecting awesome to awesome, not person to person. You're not connecting to who you know ... you're connecting to the grand possibility they are, calling the vastness of them into reality. You're a catalytic alchemical influencer who has the privilege of kickstarting a new possibility of them into reality.

HOW TO TRANSFORMATIVELY CONNECT:

1. I recommend that you never connect on the level of problem. You can listen to their story, listening for clues, breadcrumbs on the pathway to greatness ... but don't buy into the story and don't believe the version of themselves they're projecting. In front of you stands one of the most awesome beings on the face of the universe, just waiting to be seen, discovered, and called into reality. It's your job as a transformational agent to see them into being, to call their greatness into the game of Life. To believe in them so profoundly, despite all the odds, that the ripples of possibility shout hurray throughout the universe for their becoming.

2. Take a deep breath and allow yourself to expand.
Imagine you're as big as the cosmos and then let go of any sense of yourself to be ready to meet the face of AWESOME!

3. Close your eyes, raise your vibe (think of something you love) and then imagine this person in front of you ... not as you know them. Give them a gigantically huge space to be more than you can ever know.

4. Then call their greatness into that space to watch them grow. Be willing to be amazed by them, breathtaken, surprised, lifted up by the wonder of them, taken to a new space of you because you have come into contact with their greatness. In a way, it's more like you are transformed by touching their brilliance, but they are also brilliantly and awesomely transformed by your seeing. It's a win/win at a grand level, although your pure intent is solely for them to become who they are meant to be with no expectation of outcome.

In the true power of awesome connection, we are alchemical catalytic sparks that light up the realms of being, transforming it into a grand playground of becoming. We are doing something more than a transformative act for just one person. We become grand creative forces for the transformation of being at every level and for everyone. We soar into a state of transformative motion that has no rules, no step by steps, just the awesome exploration of the wonders of who is there — waiting to become what will transform us all!

Connect awesome to awesome with someone today and experience the wonder of this yourself!

Day 13

TRANSFORMATIVE POWER #5:

The Power of Exhilarating

The power to exhilarate Life is wonderful beyond compare. It requires that you ...

(1) fall wildly in love with Life,
(2) allow yourself to be a nexus point for the limitless energy of Creation to flow through you and into Life, and
(3) have a desire to GROW things wildly, wondrously, beyond imagining!

It's about bringing things ALIVE. It's about you becoming a source for the MORE'ness of Life that wants to happen through each person, the natural world, the universe, etc.

Let's start by connecting to the thriving, pulsing, limitless flow of Creation. Breathe it in and let it flow through you. Let it light you up from the inside out and the outside in. Don't try to contain it all within your body. It's bigger than that. Let yourself become a nexus pulse point for the flow. As this flow of Creation moves through you, enhance it, enrich it, power it into reality, add your genius to its potentiality, and make wonders from it.

Here's an example of that: I'm looking at a pink budding tree in my back garden right now. As I breathe in its wonder, I pulse out its super brilliance so that it can become MORE than it's ever dreamed of being, more than its 'DNA' can allow. I don't know what MORE it's going to become. I'm simply its pulse of possibility being brought more to life! I'm engaging its alive'ness and adding the powerful energy of Creation to its becoming. The sky becomes more blue for your seeing of it. The trees and flowers become more beautiful from your deep sensory engagement with them. Animals show up as awesome beings guiding us to remember the natural force that lies within all things. And people become who they really are at the deepest, most profound, expansive levels of themselves.

The true power of exhilarating someone or something into their MORE'ness is your willingness to be awed, to be breathtaken, to have the hair stand up on your arms and your jaw to drop from the sheer wonder of them.

Try it out for yourself ... first with a plant or flower, then with an animal or a person you love. Like the last piece on the power of connection ... it's Awesome meeting Awesome. But this time you're the spark, the fire, the power, the momentum of Life exhilarating itself into brilliance and beyond!

I will say that it just seems to happen of its own accord when the moment is there for it. It's not something you force into play, it's something you source in partnership with Life, with the living being you're connecting with, and with the living force that inhabits all things.

I believe that everyone wants to grow, to become more, to be alive with the exhilaration of Life! Maybe that's not true, but it sure is an awesome belief to walk around in life with, partnering with the forces of Creation to bring us to where we've never been before! Of course there are many levels of this, so play away as it feels right for you to. And remember ... **perhaps you are the limitless creative force finding expression today to bring the world into the MORE'ness it has never been before!**

Day 14

TRANSFORMATIVE POWER #6:

The Power of Genius Creation

Everyone has genius within them just bursting to get out. And genius sits in the air all around us just waiting to be brought through. It's when we marry this inner unique genius with the genius possibilities that exist all around us, that we truly see genius creation thrive!

GENIUS CREATION is about bringing through the NEW -- tapping the genius flow of limitless possibilities and creating beyond what's been known before. You could say it's about streaming the MORE'ness through for the world as a whole! It's a transformative act that transforms the world as we know it!

In genius creation, there is no imposition of will, no eruption of ego, not even an expectation of outcome. Genius creation is a thrill that excites the essence of your life -- an exuberance that lights you up from the inside out.

To create the genius NEW:

1. **Get yourself into a good high vibe (think of something you love) and get into a great relationship with the genius universe.**

2. **Surrender into the genius flows of Creation and call the NEW to you.**

3. **Allow the energy of possibility to flow to you and through you. Make a relationship with it even if you don't know what it is yet.**

4. **Dance with its energy and generate its consciousness, language, and form. Make it into a field of living reality for others to play within.**

You can do this by yourself, but doing this with others as a super conscious collective is one of the most amazing, breathtaking things you can do. For me, co-creating the genius consciousness of this planet and co-sourcing a genius universe with my super buddies has given me the most outstanding moments of my life.

If you'd like more on how to access your own genius, check out our video and audio on line learning programs to 'Discover the Genius You' www.thevisionarynetwork.com/the-genius-game.html

What does genius creation have to do with the transformation game?

TRANSFORMING YOURSELF: When you allow yourself to live and create in the flow of genius, you discover that you are so much more than you thought you were. You discover that anyone and everyone can bring through genius possibility and enrich the world with it. When you live in the genius streams you discover a love of Life, an amazing connection with the grand forces of Creation, and an ability to invent what has never been before. You make a permanent connection with the MORE'ess of Life and begin to stream that through as genius creation.

TRANSFORMING OTHERS: When you allow genius to flow through you, whether that's in words, voice, music, dance, art, invention, innovation or any other form, it stirs the world -- it moves people into a space where they are touched by something profound and vast -- and it awakens them to their own connection and genius possibility. It provides the alchemical impetus to activate the transformation.

TRANSFORMING OUR WORLD: I believe that the Earth and the universe wait with baited breath for us to 'get it' ... to initiate the movement of possibility, to direct the flows of Creation, to activate the wonders of ourselves, this world, and beyond. When we surrender into a relationship with the genius universe, we become genius creators with very little effort on our part and the MORE'ness of Life comes powering on through, rippling the world with its wonders of miraculous creation!

Day 15

TRANSFORMATIVE POWER #7:

The Power of Consciousness Creation

Consciousness, contrary to popular belief, is not a static warehouse of knowledge (past, present, and future). Consciousness is the living fabric of Creation, home of the living force, birthplace of possibility. I'm talking about 'may the force be with you' kind of force -- the creative impetus of a universe in motion, the birthplace of genius, the playground of Creation.

Most people think that you go to consciousness like a library and access its ancient information. But over the past decade, in the Visionary Network, we've been enhancing the skill of CREATING CONSCIOUSNESS, bringing it alive, and pouring it into living reality for all to create within.

This is possibly the most transformative skill one can use to transform our world. Instead of fighting against what is or trying to change things to something better -- try creating the brilliant NEW consciousness that you want to see thrive throughout the world.

Creating consciousness tends to be a collective art form, bringing the very best that each person has to offer into the creation game. I'll use a real life example below to show you how it's done ...

Two years ago in a collective creation event in Australia, we created the consciousness of a new us -- enhancing the potentiality and possibility of the human race:

1. We poured the energy, the genius, the sparks of all that we dreamed we could be into a birthing pot of consciousness.

2. We energised it as a field of possibility of us and brought it alive.

3. We made our own conscious relationship with this as the living possibility we are, and embodied it within ourselves to make it real.

That was 2 years ago and today I can see that consciousness thriving in myself, in my friends, and in people I've never met before. I can see the change in us as a race of creative, kind, caring, genius beings partnering with a miraculous genius planet.

You can create the consciousness of new business, new relationship to money, new learning, etc., etc. It's about learning to create living fields of conscious creation and making that the living space (the consciousness) in which we all thrive. It's an incredible, awe inspiring experience to be able to do this with others who share your passions and visions for the NEW.

It's an alchemical art, using consciousness as the malleable fabric of creation, aligning with the living force to make us into the limitless possibilities that we can become now.

Day 16

TRANSFORMING OUR WORLD

A Brand New Us!

I believe we are metamorphing into something we've never been before. Yes I know, some could say 'There's nothing new in the universe.', but I believe the universe is made up of an ever NEW'ing force of Creation and one of our greatest joys can be bringing through that NEW!

So how are we different today than we were 2 decades ago?   What are we transforming into?

I believe we've gone from an individualised race of beings, all separate, with many disconnected from the source of themselves, and generally disconnected from the living force of Creation. But today, so many people that I know and see in the world are full of wonder, curiosity for the NEW, excitement for the possibilities that life holds, ready to bravely go where no one has gone before.

We're connected ... to ourselves, to others, to Life, and to a wondrously enchanted Earth. We operate from knowing, tapping the genius streams, bringing through new creations in hyper speed fashion. We're visionaries, agents of transformation, difference makers extraordinaire! We don't make a big fuss of that. We don't need people to know we're doing it. We do it because we are filled with the compulsion of a universe in creation, an urging to grow beyond known boundaries to discover ourselves as we've never been before.

We're willing to evolve the very nature of being, to dance in the celebration of Life together, to weave a genius world where everyone is celebrated, honoured, and treasured as a unique contributor to the whole.

We walk lighter upon this world, raising our vibration, endeavouring to see everything from the place of potential and possibility. Our touch is magical, our words inspired by a divine urging, our creations pulled out of the oceans of possibility and laughed into reality.

We are willing to SEE every single person as amazing, extraordinary, brilliant beyond belief. We gasp in awe at their brilliance and draw that brilliance from them through our willingness to listen their genius and treasure their contribution. Are there some challenges with this? Of course. But we're committed. We see and hear the world with transformative eyes and genius ears.

We know we are becoming the living force -- thrilling every moment to the exhilaration of Creation. And in that knowing, in that exhilaration is the birthing of a brand new us!

Day 17

TRANSFORMING OUR WORLD

Creating / Sourcing Reality

Ah reality creation...one of my favourite topics. Transforming reality (yours and the world's) is an amazing transformative skill. It's a little bit like creating consciousness, but with its own distinct pizzazz!

CREATING REALITY is about energetically aligning yourself to what you want your life to look like and then manifesting that as expressions of creational magnificence. When you're creating your own reality, you're building fields of energy and consciousness for your life that translate pretty quickly into actuality. I do daily energetic exercises to call new friends, abundance, ideas, and genius flow to me. It only takes minutes and looks something like this:

1. Get in the high vibe (think of something you love).

2. Reach out with all of you to energise the living field of you.

3. Call your people to you. See your field filled with a flow of great energy, abundance, new ideas, streaming genius, and whatever else you'd love your life to be filled with now.

4. See / feel / sense it as done. There is only this reality for you from now on. Then smile knowing it's so and that it will show up to you any moment now.

Do this 2-3 times a day and see what happens. It only takes seconds to do. It's not like a meditation where you have to sit in it for a long period of time. In fact, I find the quicker you are with it, the better. You have less time to 'think' about it that way. It's about giving your life a zing every single day, sparkling it up with the reality you want now. I always find that, as long as you don't undo it with your thoughts or doubts, some form of that reality will manifest for you within a few hours or days.

SOURCING REALITY is about becoming the living force ('may the force be with you' kind of force) and holding/creating/sourcing the field of reality for all. When you're sourcing reality, you become the field of ALL / everything and source that which Life wants reality to show up as now. You birth and then stand as that greater field making sure it's tended, nurtured, and powered into global reality. Here's generally how to get there:

1. **Surrender yourself into the awe and wonder of the universe in Creation.** Let yourself be moved, breathtaken, stirred in motion with its brilliance. The feeling aspect of this is essential for without it there is little or no movement.

2. **Breathe the power of that movement (what Life wants to power into this world's reality now) through you and pulse it out into the world.** See it charming Life, dancing into the very cells of Nature, the Earth, and people the world over. Let it exhilarate Life and enchant Creation into becoming ever more.

3. **Stand at the centre point of that pulse of power and let the field of that new possibility weave into a brilliant field of consciousness that is in the very air we breathe.** Feel its strength, its wonder, its power to enchant Life and be sure to celebrate its birth.

4. **Then know that you are the source for that field and be sure to energise it, tend it, nurture it every day until one day you find that it has become itself and you can step brilliantly away to let it soar into its own adulthood as living reality.**

There comes a moment where you surrender your own reality creation to the power of the force creating awesome reality for all. You become an alchemist of Creation, an agent of transformation, a source for new reality based on limitless possibility. You become a possibilitizer (couldn't resist the new word).

Sourcing reality for all with Life, dancing as and with the force of Creation, is one of the most spectacular things I have ever done. I think my creational buddies who do this collectively along side me would agree. Surrendering to the living force of Creation will make you into an extraordinary being with breathtaking moments of splendiforous creation. The grand forces move through you, lighting up Life in wondrous new ways. You soar, you dance, you're uplifted like never before. Because the universe runs on limitless Creation and when you align with that, your reality and the world becomes something spectacularly more every single day!

Give it a go. Try creating your own reality and then sourcing reality for all and see what happens as you do each of these. What's the difference between the two? And what wonders have you sourced for us all to grow into?

Day 18

TRANSFORMING OUR WORLD

Our Metamorphic Future

The way I see it, there are four distinct types of transformation:

1. the fulfilment of potential (what you essentially already are that's just waiting to be expressed)

2. being fuelled and filled by greater purpose, reaching beyond who you've known yourself to be to become someone greater

3. death / rebirth: giving up all that you are and have been to metamorph into a brand new, never been before, YOU!

4. the metamorphosis of a race of beings, a world, and a universe into levels upon levels of genius possibility.

We're stepping into a moment of time where we're being filled with the wonder of Creation, the awe of Life in its grand motion, the limitless possibilities of us poised on the horizon of a future never seen before!

WHAT IS THIS FUTURE WE'RE METAMORPHING INTO?

A world that celebrates every single person as a genius creator, bringing something uniquely and awesomely brilliant into the game of our collective creation.

A sense of true connection with and celebration of Nature and the Earth and the Cosmos, knowing we are all part of the same fabric, knowing that how we think, act, and create ripples and uplifts the fabric for all.

A world of business that does things for the good of people and the planet, where everyone loves coming to work, able to contribute their genius to the whole.

An expansion into the stars that gives us a far broader understanding of the universe in Creation and a genius sense of transformative adventure into spaces and places unknown.

Pure connection -- that everyone is celebrated for their own unique relationship with the force of Creation, the source of Life, the divine in what ever format they embrace.

The ability to morph our own bodies into genius expression, vitality, and well-being. To live every moment of life in the pure exhilaration of possibility and creation. To know ourselves awesomely, always willing to morph to the next levels of being! To cherish every life for the genius it brings.

We are transcending the old and metamorphing into the NEW, creating Life as it has never been before. Call that future into the genius NOW! Spark the fires of transformation and exhilarate the metamorphosis so that we emerge, as a world, as a race, into something more breathtaking and spectacular than we can ever imagine! The metamorphosis of a race, a world, and a universe into a genius future now! When you tune into this metamorphic future, what do you see us becoming?

Day 19

TRANSFORMING OUR WORLD

The Transcendent YOU!

I believe we're transcending the normal human experience and moving into a whole new level of being.

Transcendent by definition means ...

Beyond or above the range of normal or physical human experience; surpassing the ordinary; exceptional; (Of God) existing apart from and not subject to the limitations of the material universe.

The transcendent you (at least so far) isn't translucent, isn't floating in the air, and isn't walking on clouds ... although it will be lovely when we do. Transcendency in its actuality is far more practical than that. It's about ...

· **sustaining a fabulous vibrational frequency all the time and in every circumstance.**

· **seeing everything that happens from a higher place with a greater purpose and then taking action** according to that potential.

· **loving Life, enhancing it in every way -- through transformative eyes and genius ears -- alivening everyone and everything -- uplifting and evolving Life as we know it.**

· **operating in conjunction with the universe n Creation -- attuned to and following the flow of what new possibilities Life wants to engage us with now.**

· **embodying expansive consciousness, streaming genius, and the living force of Creation in all that you do.**

Transcendency is about living at a completely different level of yourself, above and beyond the range of normal human experience. That is very real now and lots of people I know are now operating at this level in sustainable, practical ways.

How to get to a sustainable transcendent YOU:

1. **Keep your vibration high — always and no matter what.** Take time every day to blast some high vibe into your physical body and throughout your energy field.

2. **Stay connected.** You know the feeling of that — the flow of great energy all the way through you, the feeling of loving

Life and cherishing its brilliance. It's a breath, a sense of being awed by the vastness of forever and knowing that you are a part of its living substance.

3. See everything that happens to you from a place of greater purpose and potential. If you can't find what that is, (1) raise your vibration higher and look again or (2) ask someone else to look for you.

4. Learn to live in the streaming genius flow of you. If you want some help with that, try our Genius Game on line learning just for the fun of it. www.thevisionarynetwork.com/the-genius-game.html

5. Call the living force ('may the force be with you' kind of force) into and through you at least once a day and then allow yourself to graciously and uniquely embody that.

6. And finally begin creating from that transcendent space, bringing through all manner of new possibilities for us all. Sourcing the NEW tends to really power you into the sense of transcendent living and oh wow, does that ever feel fab!

Day 20

Riding the Waves of Living Force

There is a silent force that dwells amongst us. It sits petulantly in the air we breathe, urging us to explore its wonders, wondering why the heck we do not see or sense its power to fulfil us. It rides waves of energies, downloading streaming new'ness into and through us, pondering why we do not co-create with the genius that sparkles on the tip of every one of those waves.

It's a living force of power and genius, urging and compelling us forward on the pathway of metamorphic adventure. It is you and it is me and it is the universe powering the waves of its own creation through us.

It is infinite intelligence with a gasping grasp of knowing beyond our normal reckoning. If you allow yourself to ride the waves of this living force, you will become it and it will become YOU at the grandest of levels, beyond any previous knowing of yourself.

It is the breath of Creation, the power that drives us forward to become more and more of what we can be, sourcing a universe in infinite motion.

It is the perfection of us unfolding from the chrysalis of being. It knows us and what we're capable of beyond what we believe we can be.

If you breathe it in, it will fill you with its sparkling effervescent waves of awe and wonder and you will immediately be in touch with a world beyond this world, a reality beyond this reality, an 'otherness' version of Creation sitting side by side with the old one we've been dwelling in.

You can dwell in this other world, this reality of 'otherness'. It's a world, a reality where we don't just ride the waves of the living force, we source it, uplift it, and become it at ever evolving new levels of ourselves.

HOW TO RIDE THE WAVES OF LIVING FORCE:

1. Take a breath of deep, rich appreciation for all of Life. Breathe in the wonders of spring springing up in the world -- the awesomeness of the stars sparkling in the cosmic skies -- anything that deeply touches and stirs the wave in you.

2. Open yourself up wildly to the oceans of creation and allow its effervescent waves to flow through you, exhilarating every cell of you.

3. Now find your relationship with the living force. This is you meeting wonder, creation, and the exhilaration of Life. Make your partnership with this living force, in whatever way suits you.

4. Then if you're ready, say YES to the living force and breathe it graciously and wondrously into and through you as a gift to the world. Be sure that you're in charge of its flow so that you don't get overwhelmed by the energy. You can turn the tap up and down to increase or slow the flow in whatever way is right for you.

Do this several times a day for a month and you'll suddenly find that your knowing is instantly available, your genius is in brilliant flow, and your transformative powers are available like never before. You become an agent of transformation, a living force for Creation, an evolutionist of extraordinary visionary proportion. You become an original thinker, a brilliant creator, a genius extraordinaire ... and you walk in a world with others who do the same, having a ball co-creating the otherness of us in a brand new world.

Day 21

Seeding the Gems of Wonder

Today, we're going to wind up our transformational adventure with one last zing ... **SEEDING THE GEMS OF WONDER.**

What gets you up in the mornings? What makes life worth living? What exhilarates your days and makes your life so stunning that it fulfils you completely in every way?

The power to transform comes from a partnership with Life ... you become its steward, its catalyst, its co-creative force.

The power to transform originates in a place where Life holds its secret wonders, waiting, ever waiting for those who would brave the adventure to wander into its treasure grounds of MORE!

The power to transform requires that you take your focus off of you to place it on the ever unfolding wonders of possibility that swirl all around us in the unseen fields of genius and creation.

The power to transform will take your breath away the moment you breathe in its genius and partner with its creative propulsion.

The power to transform is yours for the asking and once you've asked, it will transform you into someone you never imagined you could be. It's a surrender of self to become a transformative agent extraordinaire, willing to always source Life into its next new becoming. Always open to the wild and wondrous waves of Creation that propel us forward into a future that we can hardly even imagine today.

On this last day of our adventure, let's take a walk on the wild side -- entering the treasure grounds of the MORE that wait for us to source Life from. It's a visualised journey, so read on and let yourself flow as you feel called ...

"Breath in the wonders of Life and know that every breath of you is more beautiful than you could ever imagine. In that breath lies the magic of Life, an elixir that will take you into places unknown. Let the breath of Life fill you up. Let your connection with the source of yourself flow through you. Let the wild waves of Creation uplift you and carry you into the stars, into the vast playground of oceanic Creation. And there in the midst of a distant star lies a portal into the treasure ground of limitless possibility waiting to be brought to Life! You glide and slide easily through the white portal of possibility and land in the land where wonders are

born. Your landing powers up white whooshes of wonder and you reach your hand to the ones that call to you. You gather these gems into you, sleeping seeds of wonder waiting to be spread throughout the universal garden. You feel them growing and stirring from your gentle caress. Then one of Life's waves picks you up and propels you home again, seeding the gems of wonder into all aspects of Life as you surf its magnificent wave. You breathe again and know you are now a part of Life's treasure unfolding into MORE and you know that you and Life will never be the same again!"

Every single person on this planet has the opportunity to partner with Life, to enhance the wonders of us, to embody the living force of Creation, and to power its transformative genius into the world. You are a transformative force of living wonder and once you know that, then everyone and everything you touch becomes more wonderful than you or they could ever imagine.

This is what can propel you from your bed every morning, what can light up your life and exhilarate your days. Walk brilliantly on the pathway of transformation and let its genius stream through you, gifting us all a world of wonders yet to be seen.

THE REAL ART OF TRANSFORMATION

Completing the Adventure

We've come to the completion of our transformative adventure. I hope that throughout this journey you've ...

- **gotten in touch with the MORE'ness of YOU,**

- **come into relationship with your transformative powers, now able to see people and the world into the next levels of who we can be,**

- **been stirred by the living force of Creation, learning to ride its exhilarating waves into transformative motion,**

- **become an agent of transformation in all that you're up to.**

If you look back to the beginning of our journey through the transformative lens, what has shifted for you over these 21 days? Do you feel more aligned with the power of transformation now?

As a final note, here's a reminder of some of the key steps to the real art of transformation:

1. Learn to see beyond 'what is'. It's about looking beyond the disguise of ordinary with radar sensing for the extraordinary that's waiting to pop into play. It's more than just 'seeing' with your eyes. It's about your willingness to engage new potential and possibility to make that come alive in people, companies and circumstances

2. Understand that everything that happens to us is pointing us towards the pathway of transformation. That will quickly reorient your view from tragedy or angst into potential and possibility. Getting stuck into problems will lock you into recycling the old. Opening things up to limitless possibility flow will bring great new ideas and exciting new possibilities into practical play.

3. Let the people you're transforming with know that they can be anything they'd like to be, that they're not the sum of their genetics, learning, and life experiences. We swim in an ocean of genius possibilities just waiting to be realised through anyone who will reach out their hand to them.

4. Here's the secret ingredient, the magic sauce: As an artist of transformation, you have to be a source for transformation to show up. You ignite it. You stir it. You fashion and shape it from the streams of potential and possibility that are flowing to and through this person, company or circumstance. It's much more than asking the right questions or pointing them in the direction of their potential. You have to realise that together you are artists of new creation and this person, company or circumstance is the canvas that Life will paint its genius upon.

It's this last piece where the real art of transformation shows up. It's about surrendering into the power of Life's transformation as the ignition point for its realisation. It's deeply touching to see possibility made real ... to play a part in igniting genius in people, businesses, and challenging circumstances.

May you walk in the wonder of Life's genius possibility, transforming everyone and everything you touch.

Find out more about our transformative, visionary, genius training at www.soleiragreen.com

CPSIA information can be obtained at www.ICGtesting.com
Printed in the USA
LVOW07s1538080315

429667LV00029B/1429/P